# Lafayette

*French Freedom Fighter*

# Colonial Leaders

**Lord Baltimore**
*English Politician and Colonist*

**Benjamin Banneker**
*American Mathematician and Astronomer*

**Sir William Berkeley**
*Governor of Virginia*

**William Bradford**
*Governor of Plymouth Colony*

**Jonathan Edwards**
*Colonial Religious Leader*

**Benjamin Franklin**
*American Statesman, Scientist, and Writer*

**Anne Hutchinson**
*Religious Leader*

**Cotton Mather**
*Author, Clergyman, and Scholar*

**Increase Mather**
*Clergyman and Scholar*

**James Oglethorpe**
*Humanitarian and Soldier*

**William Penn**
*Founder of Democracy*

**Sir Walter Raleigh**
*English Explorer and Author*

**Caesar Rodney**
*American Patriot*

**John Smith**
*English Explorer and Colonist*

**Miles Standish**
*Plymouth Colony Leader*

**Peter Stuyvesant**
*Dutch Military Leader*

**George Whitefield**
*Clergyman and Scholar*

**Roger Williams**
*Founder of Rhode Island*

**John Winthrop**
*Politician and Statesman*

**John Peter Zenger**
*Free Press Advocate*

# Revolutionary War Leaders

**John Adams**
*Second U.S. President*

**Ethan Allen**
*Revolutionary Hero*

**Benedict Arnold**
*Traitor to the Cause*

**King George III**
*English Monarch*

**Nathanael Greene**
*Military Leader*

**Nathan Hale**
*Revolutionary Hero*

**Alexander Hamilton**
*First U.S. Secretary of the Treasury*

**John Hancock**
*President of the Continental Congress*

**Patrick Henry**
*American Statesman and Speaker*

**John Jay**
*First Chief Justice of the Supreme Court*

**Thomas Jefferson**
*Author of the Declaration of Independence*

**John Paul Jones**
*Father of the U.S. Navy*

**Lafayette**
*French Freedom Fighter*

**James Madison**
*Father of the Constitution*

**Francis Marion**
*The Swamp Fox*

**James Monroe**
*American Statesman*

**Thomas Paine**
*Political Writer*

**Paul Revere**
*American Patriot*

**Betsy Ross**
*American Patriot*

**George Washington**
*First U.S. President*

# Famous Figures of the Civil War Era

**Jefferson Davis**
*Confederate President*

**Frederick Douglass**
*Abolitionist and Author*

**Ulysses S. Grant**
*Military Leader and President*

**Stonewall Jackson**
*Confederate General*

**Robert E. Lee**
*Confederate General*

**Abraham Lincoln**
*Civil War President*

**William Sherman**
*Union General*

**Harriet Beecher Stowe**
*Author of Uncle Tom's Cabin*

**Sojourner Truth**
*Abolitionist, Suffragist, and Preacher*

**Harriet Tubman**
*Leader of the Underground Railroad*

# Lafayette

*French Freedom Fighter*

JoAnn A. Grote

Arthur M. Schlesinger, jr.
Senior Consulting Editor

Chelsea House Publishers

Philadelphia

**Produced by** 21st Century Publishing and Communications, Inc. New York, NY. http://www.21cpc.com

CHELSEA HOUSE PUBLISHERS
**Production Manager** Pamela Loos
**Art Director** Sara Davis
**Director of Photography** Judy L. Hasday
**Managing Editor** James D. Gallagher
**Senior Production Editor** J. Christopher Higgins

Staff for *LAFAYETTE*
**Project Editor/Publishing Coordinator** Jim McAvoy
**Project Editor** Anne Hill
**Associate Art Director** Takeshi Takahashi
**Series Design** Keith Trego

The Chelsea House World Wide Web address is http://www.chelseahouse.com

First Printing
1 3 5 7 9 8 6 4 2

Library of Congress Cataloging-in-Publication Data

Grote, JoAnne A.
      Lafayette / JoAnne A. Grote.
        p.   cm. — (Revolutionary War leaders)
    Includes bibliographical references (p.   ) and index.
    ISBN 0–7910–5973–1 (hc) — 0–7910–6131–0 (pbk.)
      1. Lafayette, Marie Joseph Paul Yves Roch Gilbert Du Motier, marquis de, 1757–1834—Juvenile literature.   2. Generals—United States—Biography—Juvenile literature.   3. United States. Army—Biography—Juvenile literature. 4. Statesmen—France—Biography —Juvenile literature.   5. United States—History—Revolution, 1775–1783—Participation, French—Juvenile literature. [1. Lafayette, Marie Joseph Paul Yves Roch Gilbert Du Motier, marquis de, 1757–1834. 2. Generals. 3. Statesmen.] I. Title. II. Series.

    E207.L2 G84   2000
    944.04'092—dc21
    [B]                                                        00-031466
                                                                        CIP

# Contents

Lafayette grew up in a big mansion, like the one shown here, that had belonged to his family for hundreds of years.

# A Boy in a Mansion

On September 16, 1757, a boy was born in a mansion in France. The tiny baby was given a big name. He was called Marie Joseph Paul Yves Roch Gilbert du Motier de La Fayette.

The birth record states that the baby was "the very high and very mighty **noble** seigneur." A *seigneur* was a man who owned a large house, called a **manor**. A seigneur was also called a lord. A lord of a manor owned a lot of land around his large home. A lord could tell the people who lived on his land what to do. He was an important person. This tiny baby with the big name would one day be lord of the manor.

The baby also grew up to become an American Revolutionary War hero. He became so famous that people all over the world know him by the name of Lafayette–a version of the last part of his long name.

Lafayette had red hair and a long nose. His family and friends called him Gilbert. Other people called him the Marquis de La Fayette. That meant he was the lord of La Fayette.

Lafayette grew up in a mansion called the Chateau Chavaniac. This house had belonged to his family for hundreds of years. Before it was a house, it was a fort. The long house had a round tower at each end.

Lafayette's father was a French soldier. He and Lafayette never saw each other. Lafayette was less than two years old when his father was killed fighting in the Seven Years' War.

The Seven Years' War was a war between France and Britain. One of the things they were fighting over was which country would control North America. The United States didn't exist yet.

**The French and Indian War, which was fought in colonial America, was part of the Seven Years' War between France and Great Britain. Lafayette's father was killed fighting in the Seven Years' War.**

But people from Europe lived in the New World. The places where they lived were called colonies.

Lafayette's grandfather was also a soldier who was killed in battle. The only men in the mansion when Lafayette was growing up were servants. This is why Lafayette was considered a lord right from birth. Of course, he was too young to run the mansion. So Lafayette's grandmother took care of things for him.

Lafayette had no brothers or sisters. He did not even have many playmates. He was glad when his cousin, a little girl, and her mother came to live with them. His cousin's father had been killed in the Seven Years' War, too. The little girl was a year older than Lafayette.

The Seven Years' War ended when Lafayette was five years old. France lost the war to Britain. Even though the war was over, many French people still thought of Britain as their enemy. Lafayette thought Britain was his enemy, too. British soldiers had killed his father.

He often heard people speak of going to war again. Frenchmen said they would win the next war. Lafayette dreamed of growing up to be a brave soldier like his father. He wanted to help France win a war against Britain.

There were no schools near Chavaniac. A

priest was hired to teach Lafayette to read and write. One of his relatives spoke to the teacher when Lafayette was 10 years old. "I considered the boy to possess the type of mind which belongs to great men," the relative said.

Lafayette's grandmother taught him things he could not learn in school or from a teacher. She showed him how to be a good lord. She taught the boy that lords are members of the special group of people called nobles. They had special rights.

But along with their rights went certain duties. Lafayette's duties would include taking care of the poor farmers who lived on his land. These farmers were called **peasants**. Some lords only took money from the peasants and did not help them. Lafayette's grandmother taught him he must always take care of the peasants.

Lafayette's home was the largest house around. The peasants lived in little huts with grass roofs in the village of Chavaniac near the mansion. Only peasants paid taxes. Lafayette's grandmother collected taxes from the peasants who lived on

**Lafayette's grandmother taught him the duties of a lord, which included taking good care of the poor farmers who worked the land.**

their land. The money went to the king. She also collected rent from the peasants for the land they lived on and farmed.

But the peasants liked her. She made sure they

had seed for planting, and she cared for the sick. Watching her, Lafayette learned that poor people should not be ignored or poorly treated.

Lafayette knew he was much better off than the peasants. Peasants couldn't own land. The law didn't even let peasants bake bread from the grain they grew. They had to pay the lord to have the flour ground. Then they had to pay to have the bread baked in the lord's ovens.

Lafayette liked to play outside whenever he could. When he was eight, a wild animal was roaming the countryside around Chavaniac. It was killing people's animals. Some people thought it was a mountain lion. Others thought it was a wolf. Lafayette called it a hyena.

He wanted to show his bravery and decided to kill the hyena that was causing so much trouble. So he went into the woods and spent many days walking and searching. But he never found the beast.

In France, the most important thing in a person's life was knowing the king. To know the king, you had to be born into a special family like Lafayette's. These families were called noble families or **nobility**.

There were many positions even a man of nobility could not hold unless the king gave him permission. Lafayette wanted to be an officer in the army. A soldier could not become an officer without the king's permission. So Lafayette felt it was important to meet the king.

Chavaniac was in the country. Lafayette could not meet the king there. The king lived in the city of Versailles. He also had palaces in Paris. Lafayette's mother's father lived in one of the king's palaces in Paris. When Lafayette was 11, his mother decided it was time for him to move to Paris. He would live with his mother and grandfather in the Luxembourg Palace.

Life in Paris was very different for Lafayette. The palace was much larger than Chavaniac. For the first time in his life, Lafayette went to school with other children. He went to the College du Plessis, the best school in France. He studied

**Lafayette lived among rich people in Paris and went to many fancy balls and dinners.**

math, history, geography, French literature, the classics, and Latin. He rode to school in a carriage, even though the school was close to the palace. Nobles never walked when they could ride.

When he wasn't at school, he attended balls

and fancy dinners. There he met important people. Like all nobles, he wore a powdered wig and clothes embroidered with gold.

In March 1770, Lafayette's mother died. A few months later his grandfather died. His grandfather left all his money and everything he owned to Lafayette. The boy was only 13 years old. Suddenly he was one of the richest people in France. But Lafayette did not care. "I was conscious only of sorrow at the loss of my mother and had never been in the need of money."

Lafayette's mother's grandfather, his great-grandfather, took over the young man's care. His great-grandfather arranged for the king to make the 13-year-old an officer in the Black **Musketeers**. They were called Black Musketeers because of the color of their horses.

Lafayette liked the Musketeers. "I was all on fire to have a uniform. . . . I enjoyed the honor of being reviewed by the king and of riding to Versailles on horseback in full dress. . . . All the boys wore their swords when they were invited out to dine, and this matched well with their embroidered coats, their hair-bags, and their powdered and **pomaded** curls."

Lafayette wasn't expected to live like a soldier. Nobles only lived like soldiers during war, and France was not at war.

Lafayette's great-grandfather arranged for the boy to marry Adrienne d'Ayen de Noailles. It was common in those days for older family members to arrange the marriages of younger family members. The de Noailles family was wealthy and one of the most powerful families in France. They lived in Versailles, where the king lived, and were good friends with him. So Lafayette moved to Versailles.

A man who knew Lafayette when they were teenagers wrote that Lafayette "was rather awkward; he was tall, his hair was red; he danced without grace, he rode poorly."

But Lafayette must have learned to ride a horse well after that. One night he rode 70 miles on horseback, from Rhode Island to Boston, in seven hours. He then rode back in just six-and-a-half hours. That is a fast trip on horseback. It is not easy to ride fast on a dirt road at night without lights.

**King Louis XVI (shown here) and Queen Marie Antoinette were friends of Lafayette and his wife.**

There, Lafayette was promoted to captain. He moved to a different military group and became a student in the riding **academy**. There, he became friends with Comte d'Artois, the brother of the future king of France.

Lafayette and Adrienne got married in 1774. He was 16 years old, and she was just 15. People often married at that age in those days. The king and his grandchildren attended their wedding.

Soon after the marriage, the king of France died. The Comte d'Artois's brother became the new king. He was called King Louis XVI.

Lafayette and his wife spent most of their time going to balls, dinners, and concerts with friends. Two of their friends were King Louis XVI and his wife, Marie Antoinette.

Finally, Lafayette was living the life his mother had planned for him. He knew the king. He had enough money to buy everything he needed and live in luxury in a palace. But the only thing Lafayette really wanted to do was to be a soldier.

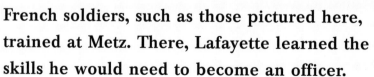

French soldiers, such as those pictured here, trained at Metz. There, Lafayette learned the skills he would need to become an officer.

# Running Away
# to America

afayette did not like the life he and Adrienne were living. He was a quiet young man and not comfortable in large crowds. He wrote in his memoirs, "I was judged unfavorably because of my silences and because I neither thought nor heard anything which seemed to me worth saying."

The soldiers trained at Metz. Lafayette enjoyed going to Metz with the military more than going to balls. The most important officer at Metz was Lafayette's brother-in-law, Comte de Broglie. Other relatives of Adrienne's were also at Metz, so Lafayette had many friends there. Best of all, he began learning the things he needed to know to become the officer he dreamed of being one day.

In August 1775, the duke of Gloucester came to Metz. He was the brother of the king of Britain. Comte de Broglie gave a dinner for the duke. He invited a number of officers, including Lafayette. The American Revolution had begun just four months earlier. The duke talked about the war. He explained why the American colonies and Britain were fighting. The duke agreed with the Americans who were fighting for their rights.

Lafayette listened closely to all that the duke said. The young man began to think that he wanted to help the colonies. From that moment, he could think of little else but offering his assistance to the Americans. He thought their struggle for freedom was important. But he could not go to America right away. He was only 17. He and Adrienne were expecting a baby. In December 1775, their daughter Henriette was born.

About the same time, the American Congress had sent a man named Silas Deane to France.

Deane's job was to convince the French to help America in the war. Lafayette finally met with Deane in December 1776. He told Deane that he wanted to fight with the Americans. Deane reminded Lafayette that the Americans were not winning the war yet. "Let us not give up our hope," Lafayette responded. "It is precisely in time of danger that I want to share whatever fortune may have in store for [the Americans]."

Lafayette meant what he said. He bought a ship and named it *La Victoire*, which is French for "the victory." He asked other officers to go to America with him on his ship. Many Frenchmen were still angry at Britain because France had lost the Seven Years' War. They wanted to fight with the Americans against Britain. It would give them a chance to beat their old enemy.

King Louis XVI found out about Lafayette's plans. He did not want Lafayette to go to America. The French king wanted the Americans to win, but he did not want France to be forced into another war with Britain.

**Lafayette bought a large warship like this one and asked other officers to sail with him to America.**

Lafayette was one of the richest men in France. The king reasoned that if Lafayette went to America to fight against the British, it might make King George III of Britain mad at France. So Louis XVI sent a message to Lafayette, ordering the young man to stay in France.

Before he received the official message, Lafayette heard rumors that the king would order him to stay. If he received an official order, he could not disobey the king. That would get him in big trouble. Lafayette had an idea: if he didn't get the message, he could still go. So he disguised himself. The king's messengers could no longer recognize him and Lafayette never received the king's order.

First, Lafayette had his ship sail to a port in Spain. Then, he traveled across land to meet his ship. On April 20, 1777, 19-year-old Lafayette left for America on the _La Victoire._ Once on the ship, Lafayette wrote Adrienne a letter. He told her how hard it was to leave her and Henriette. He loved them very much.

It took 54 days for the ship to reach the coast of South Carolina. _La Victoire_ arrived on June 13. The men on the ship had never been to America. They did not know where they could land their ship safely. Lafayette and some other officers took a small boat to shore to find someone to help them.

The first people Lafayette met in America were black men. They were fishing for oysters in the inlet. They said they were slaves of Major

Benjamin Huger, an American army officer. The slaves took the French officers to Huger's house.

Huger invited the French officers to stay overnight. The next day, he gave Lafayette and another French officer two horses and told them how to reach Charleston. The officers without horses had to walk 15 miles to reach the town.

Once in Charleston, Lafayette used almost all his money to buy carriages and horses for himself and the other French officers. They would ride to Philadelphia. The American Congress met in that city. The French officers had to meet with the president of Congress before they could join the American army.

Meanwhile, *La Victoire* hit a reef while leaving Charleston Harbor and sank. The warship that had cost Lafayette so much money would never help America win a battle.

Lafayette might not have known this when he left Charleston. It could take days or weeks for news to reach people. The roads in the colonies were poor. Sometimes they were little more than

**Lafayette's trip from Charleston to Philadelphia took a month because many roads were rough, muddy paths through forests or swamps.**

paths through swamps or woods.

One of the officers with Lafayette kept a journal. "Four days later, some of our carriages were reduced to splinters," he wrote. "Several of the horses, which were old and unsteady, were either worn out or lame, and we were obliged to buy others along the road. This outlay took all our money."

He described how they had to leave behind

much of their luggage. Some of it was stolen. They walked much of the way. Often, they slept in the woods. They were very hungry and hot. Many of them were sick with high fevers and **dysentery**. "At last," he wrote, "after thirty-two days of marching, we arrived at Philadelphia."

In Philadelphia they went to see John Hancock. Hancock was the president of Congress. He told the men to meet him at Independence Hall the next day. But the next day, they weren't allowed into Independence Hall. They were told to wait in the street outside. Finally, someone came to them and said, "It is true we were in need of officers last year, but now we have experienced men and plenty of them."

Lafayette could not believe it. He'd bought a ship with his own money. He'd hidden from the king. He'd traveled for 54 days on the ocean and 32 days over land to reach Philadelphia. He had lost his ship, carriages, and luggage. After all that, he was being told to go home.

He decided not to return to France right away.

**Lafayette was excited to arrive in Philadelphia, but he was upset when Congress rejected his offer to serve in the army.**

Instead, he wrote a letter to Congress. "After the sacrifices I have made in this cause, I have the right to ask two favors at your hands: the one is, to serve without pay, at my own expense; and the other, that I be allowed to serve at first as a volunteer."

Lafayette and his friends did not know it, but there was a good reason they had been asked to go home. Many other French officers had already asked to be officers in the American army. Most of those officers did not actually want to fight. They only wanted the title and the pay. George Washington and other Americans felt that was not fair to the American soldiers. The American officers fought hard and risked their lives in battles. Washington believed these Americans should be made officers instead of the French.

The Americans had not forgotten the French and Indian War, either. Back then, Americans had fought with the British against the French. The Americans were not sure they could trust their old French enemies to help them fight.

Lafayette also did not know that King Louis XVI had issued an order that any French officers who went to the American

L etters and papers from Lafayette's time often spell his name two different ways. Lafayette himself spelled his name both *La Fayette* and *Lafayette*. The common French spelling was La Fayette.

After 1789, he almost always signed his name Lafayette. Some people believe this was a way he showed that he did not think he was better than other people.

colonies to fight, "especially the Marquis de La Fayette," were to return at once to France.

Lafayette was well-known in France. But in America, no one knew he was a wealthy man who belonged to a very powerful family. Americans simply knew he was only 19 and had never fought in a battle. Lafayette had brought letters from other important people to tell the Americans who he was. Congress read these letters along with Lafayette's letter.

When they learned how important Lafayette was in France, the members of Congress changed their minds. Congress gave Lafayette the title of major general in the American army. He would not be put in charge of other soldiers and he would not be paid. But he could fight with the Americans.

Lafayette agreed. He hoped to prove himself to Congress. He thought that after he did, they would let him lead other soldiers like a real officer.

In this portrait, Lafayette wears a handsome officer's uniform. But he was not afraid to run into battle with his soldiers, whom he told to fight bravely.

# Fighting for America

In the summer of 1777, Lafayette met General George Washington in Philadelphia. Washington was in charge of the American army, and he invited Lafayette to stay with him. He thought of the young French officer as one of his military family. Lafayette was delighted.

Washington knew that French soldiers were well trained. They had nice uniforms and good weapons. The American army did not have these things because Congress did not have money to pay for them. Some French officers looked down on the American soldiers because of this. Washington told Lafayette, "It is somewhat embarrassing to us to show ourselves to an officer who has just come from the army of France." Lafayette said, "I am here to learn, not to teach." Washington liked his answer.

The American soldiers had very little, but Lafayette admired their courage. He wrote about this in a letter to his wife. "About eleven thousand men rather poorly armed, and much worse clad, presented a singular appearance," he said. "The best garments were a sort of hunting-shirts, loose jackets made of gray linen. . . . In spite of these disadvantages, however, they were fine soldiers and led by **zealous** officers."

Lafayette did not have long to wait to fight. The British were winning the war. They had captured New York City. Now they were coming to take Philadelphia. It was Washington's duty to protect the city. In September, his soldiers met the British soldiers in the Battle of Brandywine.

Brandywine was a small river in the hilly countryside near Philadelphia. There were only a few places where it was shallow enough to cross the river. These places were called fords. Washington moved most of his soldiers to Chadd's Ford. He thought the British would try to cross the river there. Other soldiers were sent to guard the other fords up and down the river.

About 11,000 American soldiers fought at Brandywine. Lafayette was in the front lines of the fighting. He jumped off his horse and ran among the soldiers. He urged them to move forward and fight bravely. Suddenly another officer saw blood pouring out of Lafayette's boot. Lafayette had been hit in the leg with a **musket ball**. He had been so busy fighting that he had not realized he had been wounded.

A soldier helped him get back on his horse. Lafayette and the other soldiers kept fighting. Soon, however, the British began winning the battle. The Americans had to retreat to save themselves. They moved back 12 miles. Lafayette stayed with them, trying to keep his soldiers together. He had only a few moments to stop and wrap a

**At the Battle of Brandywine, Lafayette was shot in the leg. But he did not stop fighting until the battle was over.**

bandage around his leg to stop the bleeding.

The soldiers were frightened. "In the midst of this horrible confusion, and with the growing darkness of the night," Lafayette wrote, "it was impossible to recognize anybody." Finally they came to a bridge. Soon Washington rode up. It was only then that Lafayette agreed to let a doctor look at his wound.

The Americans lost the Battle of Brandywine. More than 1,000 Americans were killed, wounded, or taken prisoner. The American soldiers could not save Philadelphia from the British army. The members of Congress left the city before the British took over the town.

For the next few months, Lafayette could not fight. He had to wait for his wound to heal. While he waited, he wrote to Adrienne about the battle. "Let me begin by telling you that I am well," he said, "because I shall have to tell you later that we had a battle yesterday in good earnest and that our side did not get the best of it. . . . The English gentlemen paid me the compliment of a musket-ball, which wounded me slightly in the leg. But it is nothing serious, dear heart."

In another letter, Lafayette wrote, "When [General Washington] sent his surgeon-in-chief to me, he directed him to care for me as if I were his son, because he loved me as much."

Lafayette wanted to get back to the battle

**Lafayette (standing at Washington's left elbow) looks on as George Washington and his officers plan the next battle. The two men had great respect for each other.**

before his wound had healed. When Washington learned of this, he wrote the young man a letter. He warned Lafayette that he must wait until he had completely healed.

While Lafayette was recovering, the American army won its most important battle of the war so far, at Saratoga, New York, in October 1777. The Americans captured more than 5,000 British soldiers.

Lafayette couldn't wait to get back into action. He joined the army three days after the British surrender at Saratoga. His wound had not healed. He could not even wear a boot on the injured leg.

A month later, Lafayette led about 300 soldiers to find out where the British troops were and what roads they were using. He saw the British soldiers moving food and supplies across the Delaware River into Philadelphia. Warships in the river were guarding the thousands of British soldiers. Lafayette and his men had to be careful not to be seen.

Later that day, one of Lafayette's scouts saw a group of about 400 **Hessians**, German soldiers who were helping the British fight the Americans. Lafayette decided to attack them.

He sent some of his soldiers to scout out

different parts of the land around them while the other soldiers fought. He told the scouts to be on the lookout for the enemy. He did not want British or Hessian soldiers to surprise them from behind. Lafayette wanted his men to be able to get away if they did not win the battle.

As it turned out, they did win. Between 50 and 60 Hessians were wounded or killed. Some were taken prisoner. Only one of Lafayette's men was killed. Five were wounded. The battle showed Washington and other American officers that Lafayette was more than just a brave fighter. He was a wise leader in battle.

Washington sent a report to Congress about Lafayette and his battle. On December 1, 1777, Congress decided Washington could put Lafayette in charge of a division of the American army. Lafayette was very excited. He asked to be put in charge of soldiers from the state of Virginia. Washington agreed.

Lafayette had more good news that December. He learned that he had another daughter. His

**The winter at Valley Forge was very hard for the soldiers because they didn't have enough food, warm clothes, or boots.**

second daughter, Anastasie, had been born in July.

Winter was coming. Things grew much worse for the American soldiers, who were camped at Valley Forge, near Philadelphia. Lafayette wrote, "They had neither coats, nor hats, nor shirts, nor shoes; their feet and legs froze till they grew black." It was bitterly cold, and the snow fell. Days would pass without the army having any food to eat. The soldiers had a problem with weapons, too. One officer at Valley Forge said, "The arms at Valley Forge were in a horrible condition, covered with rust, half of them without **bayonets**, many from which a single shot could not be fired."

About 2,500 of the 10,000 American soldiers at Valley Forge died that winter. Most of them did not die in battle. Rather they died of cold, hunger, and illness. Another 2,300 left the American army. Some joined the British army in Philadelphia, where they would have food and clothes.

The hard winter finally passed. Soon the Americans had good news. In May 1778, they learned that France and the United States had signed a **treaty**. This meant France would help the Americans by providing money, supplies, warships, and soldiers. With the help from France, the Americans would have a very good chance of winning the war. Washington told Lafayette the news. It is said that Washington told Lafayette, "You have done more than anybody to bring about this great event."

Lafayette gathered all the other French officers together to celebrate. He was proud that his country was sending help to America. He added a white sash to his uniform, which meant he was fighting for France as well as America.

Washington gave orders for how the army would celebrate. He said that 13 cannons would be fired, one for each of the American states. Then all the army's muskets were to be fired one at a time. "Upon a signal given, the whole army will huzza [shout], *Long live the King of France.*" Then the cannons were to be fired another 13 times. After that, the muskets would be fired again. Next the army was to yell, "Long live the friendly European Powers." Then the cannons were to be fired 13 more times and the muskets fired for the last time. Finally, everyone would yell, "The American States."

Lafayette was put in charge of part of the army during the celebration. Afterward, Washington announced the celebration had "afforded him the highest satisfaction." Washington was so grateful for France's help that he later hung a picture of King Louis XVI in his house.

Not all Lafayette's news was good. Right after he heard about the treaty, he found out that his oldest daughter, Henriette, had died.

The British soldiers also heard the news about France joining the war. They were not happy. They had been sure they would win the war. But America had a powerful friend in France. The French had a strong navy and well-trained soldiers.

Washington thought the British would leave Philadelphia soon because France had entered the war. If the French sent warships up the Delaware River, the British warships would be trapped.

Washington gave Lafayette a very important job. The young officer was to find out if the British were leaving and where they were going. The general ordered Lafayette to find "trusty and intelligent spies" who could tell him what was really happening. Then Washington said one more thing. He warned Lafayette not to engage his men in battle unless he really had to. The Americans could not afford to lose more soldiers.

Lafayette set out on his assignment. With him were 2,200 soldiers, including about 50 Iroquois Indians. Two days later, Lafayette found a spy. She was a young woman. Lafayette's plan was for her to go to Philadelphia to visit relatives. Then she could find out what the British were planning to do and report to him. British soldiers weren't likely to suspect a woman of spying.

Lafayette was telling the woman what he wanted her to do when some soldiers ran up to him. They were frantic. They told Lafayette that the British had seen them. About 5,000 British soldiers were going to attack. The 2,200 Americans were almost surrounded. Lafayette had to think quickly. Washington had told him not to lose more soldiers. But the situation looked like almost all of them would be taken prisoner.

There was only one place the British hadn't reached yet. Lafayette quickly sent most of his men through that hole in the British lines. He had a few small groups of men fight with the British to distract them and keep the escape route open. Most of his men got away. Only nine of Lafayette's men were killed or captured. Lafayette did not find out when or where the British were going, but he saved almost all the soldiers under his command. Washington wrote to Congress, telling them what a good job Lafayette had done.

Soon, the British army left Philadelphia. They planned to go through a village in New Jersey named Monmouth Court House on their way to New York. When they left Philadelphia, they filled the road for as far as the eye could see. A total of 12,000 British soldiers marched toward New York. The wagons alone, carrying their supplies, stretched for 12 miles.

The Americans confronted and fought the British at Monmouth. It was the longest battle of the war and neither side really won. Lafayette and his men took part in the great fight. Lafayette fought alongside Washington,

**Lafayette (on white horse, at right) rides behind George Washington at the Battle of Monmouth. Neither army was a clear winner there.**

and afterward he wrote, "never have I beheld so superb a man."

It wasn't long before French warships arrived in America. Lafayette told how he watched a battle between the French and British ships. The French ships won. "It was the proudest

**French warships like these arrived in America to help in the war against Britain.**

day of my life," he said.

After France entered the war, Lafayette decided to go back to France. He wanted to talk to King Louis XVI and find out what plans the king had for the war. The Americans were so thankful for Lafayette's help that they supplied a warship to take him back to France in January 1779.

Congress wrote a letter to King Louis XVI. It said that Lafayette was "wise in Council, gallant in the Field, and Patient under the hardships of War."

Washington also sent a letter to Benjamin Franklin. Franklin was working for America in Paris at the time, trying to get more help from the French government. Washington's letter told about the many things Lafayette had done for the American army. It talked about his battles and the wounds he had received. It described what a skilled leader he was. It even told the story of how, when almost completely surrounded, he outsmarted the British and got his troops safely away. "I have a very particular friendship for him," Washington wrote.

Lafayette was not going home to take a vacation, however. He would continue his fight for America while in France.

Lafayette returned to Paris to continue the fight for America's freedom. The French people were very proud of him and had many parties in his honor.

# To France
# and Back

King Louis XVI had not forgotten that Lafayette had gone to America against his wishes. When Lafayette arrived in France, he was put under house arrest for eight days. That meant he could not leave his house in Paris. He could not see anyone except his relatives. It was a punishment because he had not obeyed the king. Lafayette wrote the king a letter, apologizing for disobeying him.

The French people did not care that the king had punished Lafayette. They welcomed him back warmly. They had heard of Lafayette's success in America. They gave him many fancy parties. He became one of the most popular men in France.

Lafayette used his popularity to help America. He met with the king and other important men in the French government. He asked them to send more soldiers and money to America. He became friends with Benjamin Franklin and John Adams, who were in France representing America.

The American Congress had a sword made for Lafayette. On it were pictures of the most important battles in which he had fought.

Lafayette was glad to see his wife, Adrienne, again. He was also happy to see their little girl Anastasie, for the first time. He missed his older daughter Henriette. But his family was growing. On December 24, 1779, the couple had a son. They named him George Washington Lafayette.

Lafayette enjoyed being with his family, but there was still work to do in America. A few months later he left for America once again. He brought good news to Washington from King Louis XVI. The king was sending more help.

In July a French general, the Count de

**Benjamin Franklin (center), who was in France representing America, became a good friend of Lafayette's.**

Rochambeau, arrived with warships and 5,000 soldiers. Washington was in charge of both the American and French armies. Rochambeau was the most important officer under Washington.

Washington and Rochambeau could not always be in the same place at the same time. Keeping in touch with each other was difficult.

Lafayette knew both French and English. So he was chosen as the person to help the French and American officers send messages to each other.

Lafayette was also put in charge of American soldiers again. But the Americans were so short on money that only half of his soldiers had horses. Lafayette's troops were called the Light Division.

All the American soldiers were still without much food or clothing and many had no shoes. Every day, Lafayette wrote letters to the leaders of the American states. He asked them for supplies. They helped him whenever they could. The states could not help enough, though. Lafayette bought a red and a black feather for each of the men in the Light Division. It was the only thing they wore to tell them apart from other soldiers.

Lafayette also bought each of his soldiers a sword. Then he ordered uniforms from France for everyone in the Light Division.

The French soldiers had uniforms. Lafayette thought his soldiers would feel more proud if they had uniforms. In Baltimore, Lafayette bought linen cloth. He convinced the women in the city to make the cloth into shirts for his soldiers.

Then Lafayette and his soldiers were sent south to fight. They protected Richmond, Virginia, from the British.

A British general, Charles Cornwallis, was in charge of the troops in Virginia. He was considered one of the best British officers. Lafayette thought so, too. He wrote to another American general, "I am devilish afraid of him."

One time, before going to battle against Lafayette's

Lafayette was excited at the chance to fight against British General Phillips in Virginia. Lafayette's father had been killed by a cannon ball. And Phillips had been in charge of the cannon in that battle.

"By a strange coincidence," Lafayette wrote, "twenty-two years later two of our cannons opened fire on the English headquarters at Petersburg, on the Appomattox in Virginia, and one of the balls passed through the house in which General Phillips was lying sick. He was killed outright."

men, Cornwallis was very sure that his British troops would win. "The *boy* cannot escape me." Cornwallis said. He called Lafayette "the boy" because Lafayette was so young. But the boy and his men escaped from Cornwallis.

Cornwallis and his soldiers were ordered to New York. The easiest and safest way to get to New York was to travel by ship. He marched his men to a place called Portsmouth where ships could easily dock. He did not expect Lafayette's men to surround Portsmouth and cut off his escape by land. But they did.

Lafayette wrote to Washington, "Should a French fleet now come in Hampton Road, the British army will, I think be ours." He meant that if the French warships came and kept the British soldiers from leaving by ship, the British would not have any way to leave Portsmouth.

The French ships did not come. Neither did the British ships. Instead, Cornwallis moved his

**British General Cornwallis made fun of Lafayette's age. But Lafayette and his men later helped defeat Cornwallis at the Battle of Yorktown.**

men to Yorktown, Virginia.

Yorktown was built on a **peninsula**, with the York River on the northern side, the James River to the south, and the Chesapeake Bay to

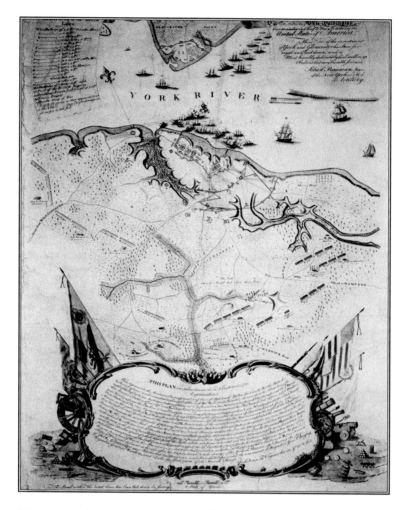

**The Battle of Yorktown (as shown in this plan) marked the end of the American Revolution.**

the east. The Chesapeake Bay was part of the Atlantic Ocean. Yorktown seemed like the perfect place for the British ships to pick up General

Cornwallis and his more than 8,000 soldiers.

Lafayette's men guarded Yorktown to keep the British from leaving by land. Cornwallis's men tried to leave Yorktown by crossing the James River, but Lafayette's soldiers stopped them.

Washington and Rochambeau were sailing for Yorktown with the French warships and more soldiers. Now it was a race. Who would arrive first? Would the British ships come and take the British soldiers off the peninsula? Or would the French warships get there first and stop the British?

The French warships were first to arrive at Yorktown. Lafayette was glad to see General Washington and the thousands of American and French soldiers. On October 10, 1781, the Battle of Yorktown began.

Seven days later, Cornwallis sent a messenger. He asked the Americans to stop the fighting. General Washington agreed. On October 19, Cornwallis surrendered. Yorktown was the last major battle of the Revolutionary War.

**The colonial army's victory at the Battle of Yorktown surprised the British, who believed they had the best army in the world.**

At noon of that day, the American and French soldiers lined the road leading out of Yorktown. The Americans were on one side and the French on the other. The line was almost a mile long. At the end of the line stood George Washington, Lafayette, and other important American officers.

The British soldiers walked between the lines from Yorktown to where the American officers were standing. The British band played a song called "The World Turned Upside Down." They chose that song because it seemed impossible to them that the poorly trained American army had beaten the best army in the world.

When it was time for the British to lay down their muskets, they turned to the French soldiers. It was too embarrassing for them to surrender to the Americans. When Lafayette saw what the British were doing, he ordered his band to play "Yankee Doodle," a song about the American soldiers. He was paying respect to them.

Lafayette later wrote to a friend, "The play, sir, is over. . . . My heart has really enjoyed the end."

When Lafayette returned to Paris, he was hailed as a hero of both America and France.

# Hero of Two Worlds

When Lafayette returned to France, he was more famous than ever. He was called the "Hero of Two Worlds." King Louis XVI gave him an important position in the French army.

Lafayette was also asked to work with Benjamin Franklin. He helped Franklin convince the king to lend America even more money.

Soon, Lafayette and Adrienne had another baby. They named their new daughter Virginie. Her name came from the state of Virginia where Lafayette's good friend George Washington lived.

In 1783, a treaty was signed in Paris between

Britain and America. It ended the American Revolution.

That same year, things were hard for the peasants in France. Crops did not grow well near Lafayette's home of Chavaniac. There was little wheat for making bread. Lafayette had stored lots of wheat. Because other people had so little of it, his wheat was worth a lot of money. His business manager told him to sell his grain. Lafayette said, "No. Now is the time to give it." He gave it all away to the peasants.

He and Adrienne tried to make life better for the peasants in other ways. They began a weaving school for them. They also built a hospital.

Even though the American Revolution was over, Lafayette continued to fight for liberty. He wanted the same rights for French people that the Americans had won in their revolution. In 1789, he wrote the *Declaration of the Rights of Man and Citizen*. It was based on the American Declaration of Independence. He asked Thomas Jefferson to read his document because Jefferson had written

**Lafayette wrote to Thomas Jefferson, and asked for his advice on his declaration of citizens' rights for France.**

the Declaration of Independence. Jefferson liked Lafayette's essay, so Lafayette presented it to French lawmakers.

People in France wanted more rights, too. Only days after Lafayette presented his *Declaration of the Rights of Man and Citizen,* the French Revolution started. Lafayette had wanted the French to change their ways of government slowly. He did not want the French people to fight and kill each other. But that was what happened.

Some French people thought all wealthy people like Lafayette and King Louis XVI should be killed. These people wanted to take all the money, land, and houses that belonged to the rich and give them to the poor.

Lafayette tried to tell the people this was not the

After the American Revolution, Lafayette wrote to George Washington. He wanted to buy farm land with Washington. Then black people could work the land and get paid, rather than being slaves.

Lafayette felt that if Washington did this, other people would do the same thing. This would make life much better for black people in America. We do not know if Washington answered his letter, but the two men did not buy a farm together.

Years later, Lafayette bought a plantation on Martinique, an island in the Caribbean Sea. Slaves were trained to run the farm. Then they were freed.

**Lafayette's friend King Louis XVI was captured and later was killed by French revolutionaries.**

way to win their liberty. For a while, he was able to protect the king who had helped America win the war. But that made some people angry.

Lafayette told the king, "Your majesty knows my devotion to the Crown, but if it separates itself from the cause of the people, I shall remain on the side of the people." He meant that if he had to choose between defending the king and bringing liberty to the people, he would choose liberty.

Finally, Lafayette had to flee from France to save his own life. But he was caught. He spent the next five years in prison. He was luckier than King Louis XVI. The king and his queen were killed along with hundreds of other members of the nobility. Adrienne's mother, grandmother, and sister were all killed.

One time, Lafayette escaped from prison with the help of two men. One of the men was the son of Major Huger, in whose home Lafayette had spent his first night in America. But he and his friends were captured and sent back to prison.

For a while, Adrienne was safe in Chavaniac, but then she was sent to prison, too.

Lafayette and Adrienne's property was sold. Finally, Adrienne was set free from prison. She sent their son to visit George Washington in the United States. She hoped that would keep the boy safe.

Adrienne asked to stay in prison with Lafayette. Her wish was granted. Their daughters, Anastasie and Virginie, went to live with them, too.

Years later, the family was released from prison. They were only able to get back some of their property. They moved to a mansion in the country called La Grange. Their son was sent back home to France to join the family. They lived at La Grange for the rest of their lives.

For a long time, people believed most of the letters of Lafayette and Adrienne had been destroyed during the French Revolution. Then, in 1955, new owners moved into La Grange, the house Lafayette once lived in.

In one of the tower rooms, they made an amazing discovery. They found hundreds of letters and other things that had belonged to Lafayette and his wife. A British woman who married one of Lafayette's grandsons had hidden the items in the tower. We have learned many new things about Lafayette and his family through these letters.

**President James Monroe invited Lafayette to visit the White House and tour America to celebrate the 50th anniversary of the start of the Revolutionary War.**

Adrienne died in 1807. Lafayette was very sad to lose his dear wife. He never remarried.

In 1824, Congress and President James Monroe invited Lafayette to visit America. The United States would be celebrating the 50th anniversary of the beginning of the American

Revolution the following year. They wanted Lafayette to help them celebrate.

Lafayette brought his son with him. They stayed a year, traveling to every state. Everywhere they went there were celebrations, parties, and dinners in Lafayette's honor. Americans had not forgotten all he had done to help them during the revolution.

On May 20, 1834, Lafayette died in Paris at age 76. He left behind 3 children, 11 grandchildren, and 12 great-grandchildren.

Americans were sad to hear Lafayette had died. America had lost a great friend, and Congress asked Americans to mourn his death for 30 days.

Americans expressed their thanks to Lafayette in many ways. One man gave Lafayette a huge white stallion. Lafayette rode it with the Light Division during the war.

After the war, the United States gave Lafayette land in Louisiana. Signs were made to mark the places where he fought. Many statues of him were also made. Counties, towns, streets, and even a college were named after him. The Revolutionary War hero Patrick Henry named a son, Fayette, after Lafayette. Lafayette and all his male descendants were made citizens of most of the states.

The American people have still not forgotten Lafayette. Every year since 1834, on May 20, the American ambassador to France has visited Lafayette's grave in Paris. The visit reminds American and French citizens that Lafayette helped America win its freedom.

# GLOSSARY

**academy**–school

**bayonet**–steel blade attached to the end of a musket or rifle

**dysentery**–an infectious disease

**Hessian**–German soldier fighting with the British during the American Revolution

**manor**–mansion with a lot of land around it

**musket ball**–bullet from a musket

**musketeer**–a soldier with a musket

**noble**–a member of a rich family or group who receives special privileges

**nobility**–a group of people with special rights; they are usually rich

**peasant**–poor farmer

**peninsula**–a piece of land surrounded on three sides by water

**pomaded**–perfumed

**treaty**–an agreement between two or more people or groups of people

**zealous**–eager

# CHRONOLOGY

| | |
|---|---|
| **1757** | Born on September 6 at Castle of Chavaniac, France. |
| **1759** | Father dies in battle during Seven Years' War. |
| **1770** | Mother and grandfather die; inherits large fortune. |
| **1774** | Marries Adrienne d'Ayen-Noailles on April 11. |
| **1777** | Sails to America; meets George Washington; made major general in United States Army; wounded in Battle of Brandywine; given command of Virginia Continentals; spends winter at Valley Forge. |
| **1778** | France and United States sign treaty in February. |
| **1779** | Leaves America for France to ask for more help. |
| **1780** | Returns to America. |
| **1781** | Helps Washington defeat Cornwallis at Yorktown; leaves America for France. |
| **1783** | Treaty of Paris is signed. |
| **1789** | Writes *Declaration of the Rights of Man and Citizen*; French Revolution begins. |
| **1792** | Captured and imprisoned in France. |
| **1796** | Released from prison. |
| **1824–25** | Visits United States for 50th anniversary of the beginning of the Revolutionary War. |
| **1834** | Dies in Paris on May 20. |

# REVOLUTIONARY WAR TIME LINE

**1765**  The Stamp Act is passed by the British. Violent protests against it break out in the colonies.

**1766**  Britain ends the Stamp Act.

**1767**  Britain passes a law that taxes glass, painter's lead, paper, and tea in the colonies.

**1770**  Five colonists are killed by British soldiers in the Boston Massacre.

**1773**  People are angry about the taxes on tea. They throw boxes of tea from ships in Boston Harbor into the water. It ruins the tea. The event is called the Boston Tea Party.

**1774**  The British pass laws to punish Boston for the Boston Tea Party. They close Boston Harbor. Leaders in the colonies meet to plan a response to these actions.

**1775**  The Battles of Lexington and Concord begin the American Revolution.

**1776**  The Declaration of Independence is signed. France and Spain give money to help the Americans fight Britain. Nathan Hale is captured by the British. He is charged with being a spy and is executed.

**1777**  Leaders choose a flag for America. The American troops win some important battles over the British. General Washington and his troops spend a very cold, hungry winter in Valley Forge.

**1778**  France sends ships to help the Americans win the war. The British are forced to leave Philadelphia.

**1779**  French ships head back to France. The French support the Americans in other ways.

**1780**  Americans discover that Benedict Arnold is a traitor. He escapes to the British. Major battles take place in North and South Carolina.

**1781**  The British surrender at Yorktown.

**1783**  A peace treaty is signed in France. British troops leave New York.

**1787**  The U.S. Constitution is written. Delaware becomes the first state in the Union.

**1789**  George Washington becomes the first president. John Adams is vice president.

# FURTHER READING

Barner, Bob. *Which Way to the Revolution? A Book about Maps.* New York: Holiday House, 1998.

Carter, Smith, ed. *The Revolutionary War.* Brookfield, Conn.: Millbrook, 1991.

Freedman, Russell. *Teenagers Who Made History.* New York: Holiday House, 1961.

Glubok, Shirley. *Home and Child Life in Colonial Days.* New York: Macmillan, 1969.

Gross, Ruth Belov. *If You Grew up with George Washington.* New York: Scholastic, 1993.

Harmon, Dan. *Fighting Units of the American War of Independence.* Philadelphia: Chelsea House, 1999.

Holbrook, Sabra. *Lafayette, Man in the Middle.* New York: Atheneum, 1977.

Mello, Tara Baukus. *George Washington.* Philadelphia: Chelsea House, 2000.

# INDEX

# PICTURE CREDITS

# ABOUT THE AUTHOR

**JOANN A. GROTE** loves to read and write about history. She has written more than 20 historical novels for adults and children. She has also written *Paul Revere* and *Patrick Henry* for the REVOLUTIONARY WAR LEADERS series published by Chelsea House Publishers. Her short stories and articles have been published in magazines, including *Teen* and *Guideposts for Kids.* JoAnn worked at the historical restoration of Old Salem in Winston-Salem, North Carolina, for five years. Today she lives in Minnesota.

Senior Consulting Editor **ARTHUR M. SCHLESINGER, JR.** is the leading American historian of our time. He won the Pulitzer Prize for his book *The Age of Jackson* (1945), and again for *A Thousand Days* (1965). This chronicle of the Kennedy Administration also won a National Book Award. He has written many other books, including a multi-volume series, *The Age of Roosevelt.* Professor Schlesinger is the Albert Schweitzer Professor of the Humanities at the City University of New York, and has been involved in several other Chelsea House projects, including the COLONIAL LEADERS series of biographies on the most prominent figures of early American history.